The Ant Farm

Introspection,

Refraction

&

Farewells

The Ant Farm

Introspection,

Refraction

&

Farewells

by

Lee Alloway

Ancient Eagle Press
Falls Church, VA

This edition of The Ant Farm has been printed in the United States of America by Ancient Eagle Press.

Copyright © 2011 Lee Alloway
All rights reserved.

For
Jenny and Holly

The Ant Farm

MEIOSIS	1
Introspection	3
BREAKFAST ON A WINTER MORNING	4
MARCH MADNESS	6
APRIL MORN	7
A THOUSAND FLOWERS	8
SUMMER LEASE	9
AUTUMN LEAVES	10
PASSAGES	11
TO PEGGY	12
GRAELING	13
ETERNAL OCEAN	14
WEDNESDAY MORNING, 3 A.M.	16
THE PACT	18
DREAMLAND	19
WHEN THE TIME IS RIGHT, TAKE MY HAND	20
BEWARE OF THE DREAMER	21
I WILL	22
WE WALK A THIN LINE, YOU AND I	23
WHAT WILL IT MATTER?	24
YOU'RE NEVER TOO OLD TO BE YOUNG	25
BARGAINING WITH GOD	26
A SOLDIER'S CHILD	28
THE SENTINEL	29
REMEMBERING THE FALLEN	31
THE DANCE OF THE FOOLISH OLD MAN	32
GHOSTS	34
SIENA	37

Refraction — 39

- The In Basket — 41
- The Zoophabet — 42
- LMRX — 50
- A Valentine's Poem — 52
- A Valentines Poem -1993 — 53
- Mango Dreams — 54
- Mothers' Day — 55
- Maddie McGuire — 56
- A Haiku in the Woods — 59

Farewells — 61

- Thantos — 63
- 92 — 64
- Death Take the Final Scene — 65
- What is the Sun without its Warmth? — 66
- If we get to the end of the road — 67
- Night — 68
- …The Now — 69
- Are you fact or fantasy — 70
- All the words unspoken — 71
- Polac Cloj — 72
- Blind Men — 73
- When first I felt the breeze caress my face — 74
- At Night She Cries — 75
- Here I am — 77

Epilogue	**79**
A Prayer on Parting	80
Charles Bridge, 1993	83

Meiosis

☐ ☐ ☐

You're back

You're back.
A different face, a different name;
The voice, the laugh in a different key,
But it is you, after all.

I know you by the way you fit into my heart

And once again I play the fool,
For once again I have the single thing I fear losing
Knowing all the while that the fear will lead
Inescapably to the losing.

And bring the healing pain

My days are measured by the hours
Waiting for your call that never comes.
My words are never spoken,
Remembering the moment that never has been.

And let my spirit sing.

And still there is you
With your imperetratable eyes,
Slipping slowly away
While my gifts lie unopened at your feet.

And fill my life with joy.

Introspection

I have an ant farm. Wanta see my ant farm? I bought it with my own money. Saved all summer. Wanna see my ant farm?

Breakfast on a Winter Morning

Snap. Crackle. Pop.
The smell of coffee mixing with the smell of smoke,
The yard's detritus snapping, crackling, popping in the fire pit.
A hawk perches in the tree, 20-feet up.
I can't see her, but I sense her.
I can hear a hundred meters east, west, south,
The morningsong of the wren, the sparrow, the dove,
But here in the yard, only the snap, crackle, pop of the fire.

Five minutes, ten, she loses patience,
Quits her perch and takes silently to wing.
Suddenly, behind me, above me, a scream.
Loud, sharp, jay-like,
A Sharp-shinned hawk.
She knifes through the trees on compact wings,
Screaming the indignity,
Of me sitting at her breakfast table.

There's ice on the pond, but I'm warm,
The coffee mug in my hands.
The fire has banished the morning chill,
And I am cocooned in the blankets of time,
The journeys taken, the losses survived,
The laughter shared, the friends who have passed,
The fears confronted, the confidences finally spoken,
Have brought me here today. They comfort me and keep me warm.

The birds return.
Chickadee and cardinal brave the safflower,
Titmouse and house finch to the sunflower seeds,
Goldfinch on the Niger,
Downy and Red-bellies stab the suet,
Junco, song sparrow, dove and wren,
Hoover the millet and insects beneath the feeders,
Blue jays find the peanuts and the feeding frenzy begins.

March Madness

March is winter's sucker hole, and gladly I dive in.
Snowdrops and crocus jewel the lawn,
Hyacinth, jonquil and tulip sniff the air,
A hint of warmth in every breeze.

The flower beds are cleaned and wear new mulch,
Fallen branches cleared and burned,
Netting off the pond,
Stirring fishes from their torpor.

The hazelnut begins to yawn,
Catkins stretching from their winter sleep,
Pendulous, languid, dancing in the wind,
Their ladies blooming scarlet, unnoticed on bare limbs.

Bikes off the rack, chains oiled, tires filled,
A month before the warblers migrate north.
On the horizon, dark clouds gather,
And springtime dreams run before the storm.

April Morn

April morn is wont to bring,
The soft, sweet smell of waking Spring,
The melow must of new-turned sod,
The mighty, molding hand of God.

The sure sown seed, the eager vine
Does swiftly from its shelter twine;
Content no longer lying there,
It leaves the womb and seeks the air.

While lovers waking in the glade
Find misty mornings Heaven-made,
The rushing rivers of the night
Now sleepy, steaming streams of light.

The forest has been born anew,
Bedecked in emerald, jeweled in dew.
The lovers kiss, and ere they part
He takes her hand, she gives her heart.

She pledges love through coming years;
Her lover yawns, he hardly hears.
Then, dull for sleep, he turns to go
And puts the vine beneath his toe.

The vine forsakes this small disdain
And starts its skyward search again,
Yet Love is made of fragile stuff
And oft expires from chance rebuff.

And so it is with man and maid.
A loving gesture ne'er repaid,
A callous act or careless eye
Can cause a growing love to die.

Or sadder yet, the morning air,
May find that Love was never there.

A Thousand Flowers

A thousand flowers bloom in my garden,
Daffodils of white, yellow and orange
Gather in crowds, stand sentry, wander the yard,
Hyacinths and tulips celebrate in a riot of color,
A carpet of purple, a cloud of white,
The pompous peony standing apart.

A thousand dreams bloom in my heart,
Smells of a Tuscan afternoon,
Evening chill on the Maasai Mara,
The fragment of a song, the promise of a fresh canvas,
Languages tonal, guttural, melodic,
A dance in the Macedonian midnight.

A thousand projects bloom on my desk,
Data to master, deals to make,
Where millions become budget dust,
And mistakes are paid in blood.
Where decades of experience,
Weigh the vagaries of the moment.

But through it all there is one.
In the beauty of the flowers,
It is your face I see,
When my dreams take me traveling,
It is you with whom I share discovery,
And you, too, bear the burden of finding the right turn in the fog.

Summer Lease

☐ ☐ ☐

These are the days I most enjoy,
Here in my summer lease by the shore,
Rain dripping from the eaves, a book in my lap,
A small fire in the pot-bellied stove.

It is Spring, ahead of the season
When the beautiful young people arrive
To show off their bodies along the boardwalk and the beach,
In the ageless mating dance that, at its heart, never changes;

When overweight fathers and vigilant mothers,
With unfocused children, sunburned and high on sugar,
Shop for saltwater taffy and tee shirts,
And postcards with pictures of some other beach;

When old people arrive with their beach chairs and memories
Of when they were those parents, or those children,
But usually, of when they were those beautiful young people,
In the ageless mating dance that, at its heart, never changes.

Autumn Leaves

I have loved you since the beginning of time,
And will love you until time comes full circle.
If we have touched for a day,
Do not grieve that we are now apart,
But rejoice that our dreams have been given substance
Until the next of our days.

We travel like the autumn leaves,
Caught in the rush of a swiftly flowing stream,
Pulled by the unrelenting call of the sea.
For a time we traveled together, were one.
If we are caught in different currents now,
Know that the oneness remains.

Passages

A season has passed since you walked these grounds.
The pond has shed her fishnets and dressed in gossamer,
Put on iris ear loops of purple and yellow,
Cinched her waist with water lettuce and hyacinth,
A water lily blooming at her cheek;
Snow bells have come and gone,
Crocus and jonquils in their wake;
May apples, trout lilies, coral bells flirted briefly beneath the oaks;
Tiny chestnut and giant peony buds flowered and delighted;
Ginger and violets, dandelions and grasses have painted the lawn,
As poplar and crepe myrtle splashed yellows and reds against the sky.
And now, as crystal summer yields to misty autumn,
I watch the world prepare for winter sleep, resting to begin again
The timeless dance across these grounds where once you walked.

To Peggy

Those were pretty times, those Sunday mornings,
When the room was warm with sunlight,
And I would lie in bed, pretending to sleep,
Listening to the sounds of you and our daughter, so excited,
Fixing breakfast "…quietly, so we don't wake Daddy."

Those were pretty times, those Sunday mornings,
When we would dress in our not-quite-finest clothes,
Put ribbons in our daughter's hair,
And go to church. I have to admit,
It was you I worshipped. Nothing higher.

Graeling

I searched the heavens and the earth,
The depths of the seas I plumbed,
And discovered its mysteries,
But in all my searching, I never found you,

Nor any treasure to match the touch of your hand,
No beauty the measure of your smile,
No music the rival of your voice,

And no pain like your rebuke,
No loneliness like your turning away,
No emptiness like days without you.

Eternal Ocean

The eternal ocean
> Sunlight dancing from the crest of her waves
> The rising and falling,
> Ebb and flow of her cradling mass.

She nurses the injured spirit
> Nurtures the poet
> Frees the captive soul
> Consumes those who would know her.

She is the mistress of us all
> Slave of the moon
> Driven by the wind
> Painted by the sky.

The eternal ocean
> Is like our love, My Love,
> The dancing sunlight of your eyes,
> The ebb and flow of our passions.

It is your being that nurses my spirit
> That fills my pen with words.
> My soul takes flight,
> Is consumed by the knowledge of you.

You are the love that my spirit serves,
> You who are slave to the stars,
> Cast like the sea spray,
> On the icy winter shore.

And like the ocean, your love cannot be captured.
> There is no ocean in a jar, only water,
> Without life,
> Without torment.

Should I possess you, my love,
> There would be no love, only possessing
> Without life,
> Without torment.

So I will love you freely
> My eternal ocean, my eternal love.
> Like the air I breathe, the sky in which I live
> You nurture me.

Wednesday Morning, 3 a.m.

Sea

You are mine.
The moon bids me rise and come to you.
I reach out, gently touching, caressing,
A whisper, a kiss, then I recede,
Always to return, to reach further,
To touch you more deeply.
With each return, I flow against your ivory plains,
And fill your valleys until all is glass.
With every force of nature I surge again,
Against your breakers I am torn,
With fury and surrender I am consumed by you.
I cleanse you, flow into you, and disappear,
As our perfect fit makes us one.
You are mine.

& Shore

You are mine.
When the moon bids you come to me,
It is I who gives you form.
I am the giver of life.
Though driven by all the forces of nature,
You come to me without structure, and conform to me wholly.
I await your touch,
I feel your caress, your breath across my skin,
I accept your given kiss, and draw you into me,
I wrap you in my nurture, until the moon bids you go.
With your passing, I glisten in the moonlight,
Your tears on my face,
Until the moon sends you back to me.
You are mine.

The Pact

We look at each other and silently agree – nothing happened.
Our eyes fall, and the world turns cold.
A wind blows. The walls are ice-luminous.
The truth tears through our hearts.

I hold your hand and say it doesn't matter,
Paying for the lie with the pain in my breast,
For if not this, nothing matters.

Afraid to let go,
You hold me with the promise of tomorrow,
I hold on to the memory of yesterday.

Dreamland

And now I am in the dream land,
That sweet land where lovers have dwelt since the beginning of time,
Where rejected lovers have come to seek rebirth of imagined love,
Here I dwell alone, seeking happiness in my dreams.

But there is no happiness in my dreams, for they are all one.
All my dreams, all my waking and sleeping dreams, are one.
It is my life and my death, my greatest joy and eternal shame,
For this dream, this all-in-one, is She.

She, who I come here to forget,
She, who was my life and yet my death,
She, who was never born, and yet took away my life,
This child, unborn, and yet my wife.

The land of dreams can hide only the failures of others,
Our own stay with us always, to haunt and torment us,
And my failure was greatest of all:
By giving up my life, I took from this beautiful child the chance to live.

When the Time is Right, Take my Hand

When the time is right, take my hand.
> Let me share with you the life you have given back to me,
> Let the joy you have awakened in me flow into your heart,
> Let me fill you with your own power.

When the time is right, take my hand.
> When you know your own heart, and I know mine,
> When tomorrow is measured in years, not in minutes,
> When the world is ripe with promise,

When the time is right, take my hand.
> And all that goes with it will be yours –
> Love and loyalty, friendship and sharing, my arms to enfold you,
> And a depth of passion that knows no bounds.

But if our time is not to be,
> If your hand cannot live in mine because I hold too tightly,
> If the intensity of my need for you frightens you away,
> If my faults are too many, the cost of loving me too high,

Know that I will love you still for the precious gifts you have given me –
> The gift of love when love was dead,
> The gift of laughter, when joy was lost,
> The gift of sharing in a way I never knew,
> The gift of your friendship. The gift of you.

When the time is right, take my hand.

Beware of the Dreamer

☐☐☐

Beware of the Dreamer, the Poet, the Schemer,
The writer of Songs,
      For his heart often longs
      For a world none can share.
           He won't welcome you there.

Beware of the Hurting, the Drifting, the Flirting,
The Crafter of Speech,
      For his grapples can reach
      To the heart of the Giving.
           Resist and keep living.

Beware of the Smiling, the Happy, Beguiling,
The Ones Who Don't Cry,
      For whom pain has passed by
      Cannot suffer your sorrow.
           They'll leave you tomorrow.

I Will

Who will take your outstretched hand,
When evening shadows fall,
And plant your pansies in the Spring,
Along the garden wall?

Who will look into your eyes,
And always feel a thrill
That lasts beyond the fires of youth?
I will, my dear. I will.

Who will know your every joy,
And share the tear you cry,
When loved ones slip beyond your reach,
And pass without good-bye?

And who will lie beside you,
When the nights are cold and still,
And be your constant comforter?
I will, my dear. I will.

For you have seen the demons
That have torn into my soul,
And with your gentle constancy,
Your love has made me whole.

So in a royal palace,
Or a cabin on a hill,
If you let me love you always,
I will, my dear, I will.

We walk a thin line, you and I

□ □ □

We walk a thin line, you and I.
Me with my emotions on the inside,
You always in search of something,
Me afraid to search.
Each of us needing each other so much,
But needing other people sometimes, too.
Are you as jealous of my others as I am of yours?
I doubt it.
You are strong enough to share.
I am weak, but you don't like that weakness,
So you ignore it - you can't cope with it any better than I can.
I write you love songs to tell you what my words can't say;
Why can't I give you the freedom to be happy?
And if I knew that freedom would make you happy,
Where would I find the strength to set you free?

What will it Matter?

What will it matter, in centuries to come,
      That we have loved tonight?
Will the grass be less green, the sun shine less brightly,
      Because we have stolen this moment?
Will nations fall, the rivers stop flowing,
      Because we have cast aside the rules?

The strength of our love, the thunder of our passion,
      Lives only within us.
         It will not be noted in the earth's tomorrows,
         Never etched on the mountain's brow.

So let us love while we love,
      And if future generations are untouched,
      We will carry the warmth of today
      Into the winter of tomorrow.

And if our passions precede us to eternal bliss,
      Today will live forever;
      We will touch each other still
      In our memories of youth.

You're Never Too Old to be Young

You're never too old to be young, my dear,
You're never too ancient to fly,
To laugh right out loud, to sing in a crowd,
To dance with your engine on high.

You're never too wrinkled to grin, my friend,
It's something we once understood,
To offer a smile every once in a while,
To a stranger can make you feel good.

You're never too fragile for love, my dear,
No matter how broken your heart,
In time you will find a friend who will bind,
The pieces back into one part.

You're never too old to be young, my dear,
Until you're too jaded to cry,
Till you get so discerning you can't feel that burning,
For new love that catches your eye.

So let us forever be young, my love,
And dance in the moonlight as one,
For the years that have passed gave us memories that last,
And the years still ahead will be fun.

Bargaining with God
□ □ □

Dear Jesus,
Help me through this week.
I really miss Mom and Dad
I feel so lost and alone,
Please make everything the same when I get home from camp.
I'll go to Sunday school every week and never hit my sister again.
(Thank you, Jesus.)

I don't know if I can do this.
What if she laughs at me?
Lord, don't let her laugh at me.
I'll be the only kid in the school without a date.
If she goes with me, I promise I'll treat her like one of your saints,
And I won't smoke or even have a beer.
(Thanks, Lord.)

This could turn out bad. Real bad.
I'm so far behind this plane, I have no business being here.
Heavenly Father, just get me home safely,
And I promise to study every Caution and Warning in the book.
I'll even memorize the hydraulic system. I swear.
(Thank you, Father.)

She is so small. What's wrong?
Nine months along and no bigger than my hand,
The priest is in the delivery room.
Not now. Not this time.
Oh, God. Make her strong. Make her healthy.
We'll raise her right. We'll love her with all our hearts.
(Thank you, God.)

Don't take her, Lord.
I'll plant bulbs every Fall, in the worst weather,
In the rain and cold, for the beauty of your earth,
Just let her live through one more Winter, till these bulbs bloom,
Don't let the cancer have its way.
I need her, Lord. Without her I am lost.
Oh, God...

There is no...God...

A Soldier's Child

My father arrived in an envelope most Wednesday afternoons.
I could feel my mother's pain when there was no mail,
No father from half a world away, whose face I could not recall,
Who was only the memory of a smell, a hug, a song at bedtime.

To me, the letter *was* my father.
His voice spoke through my mother's reading,
His hand had touched that paper, his pen had written those words
That came alive as I looked at the curves on the page,
Sent two weeks ago, answering Mother's questions of last month,
But for me, they were immediate and vital.

And Mother carried each letter in her apron pocket until the next arrived,
When last week's letter would join the others, tied with a ribbon,
Placed in a box on the dresser, where I would go when nobody knew,
To wonder at the box, and be with my father.

The Sentinel

A starless shroud has closed around, the night is cold and damp,
The sky has wept a million tears upon the asphalt ramp,
The cutting wind chills to the bone and tears the dreams apart,
But knife-edge loneliness is worse. It cuts into the heart.

Yet in the midst of wind and rain, until the mist of dawn,
The sentinel stands silent watch, a patient, passive pawn,
A man not unlike other men who laugh and love and cry,
Now walks with just his conscience and the dark, foreboding sky.

His thoughts are of his home and friends, his children and his wife,
He contemplates his usefulness, the value of his life,
He tries to while the hours away in happy make believe,
But loneliness is too intense, this cold, gray winter eve.

While other men sing joyful songs in embers' magic light,
The sentinel is forced to turn his collar to the night,
And walk along the raw red line, and strain his mind to see
How walking guard along the line can keep his country free.

While clad in concrete comfort at the passing of the year,
Six dozen waiting for the words that no one wants to hear,
Reflect upon their mission, their reverie subdued,
And sit together talking in their stonewall solitude.

And in his way each pilot, each member of his crew,
Will ask his god for courage, for the things he has to do,
And prays his steed unblemished when he leaves the circling camp,
Then thanks the Lord in Heaven for the guardians of the ramp.

Remembering the Fallen

Remembering those fallen from the footless fields of flight,
In quiet times I see them still, long absent from my sight,
The faithful friends, companions true, with love of life so strong,
Yet unafraid to live with Death, enjoying Sirens' song.

With only love of country standing over love of flight,
And love for smiling faces that could warm a foreign night,
And love of well-spent fellowship, the glass of foaming beer,
That numbs the soul's desire for home, and stems the budding tear.

Remembering the fallen, we recall – too long ago –
The dreams we shared in common of the things we did not know,
The high ideals of yesteryear, my friend, they were not wrong,
They have their place in time and space, a minstrel's musing song.

Like warriors long before us, we follow Gawain's trail,
And fling our coursers through the skies in search of modern grail,
Then seeking respite from our strife we sadly lay our heads
Upon the earth, while others sleep contented in their beds.

Remembering the fallen, I recall that I must go,
One day to join my brothers in the fretful fields below,
Or perhaps God in His mercy will redeem us from our Hell,
And let us live forever in the skies we love so well.

The Dance of the Foolish Old Man

The alarm intrudes. He stumbles from bed to shower, eyes closed.
The water falls cold on his feet, warms, steams, renews,
She joins him, they share a moment,
He departs with a hug, shaves while she rinses her hair.

He pulls on his flight suit, gloves in the pocket, knife against the thigh,
Opens his eyes…and selects a tie to match the shirt,
Makes the bed and leaves quietly, not waking his wife,
Asleep in the next room, where she fled his snoring years ago.

In the kitchen he reaches for cold pizza,
But his hand returns with organic yogurt.
He folds back the top on his roadster and drives to the airdrome,
Though it is a Prius he parks, not at the flight line, but at the office.

Morning briefings, target study, defensive countermeasures,
The Intel briefer flirting, asking if he'll be at the club on Friday,
In the blink of a lifetime turns to an e-mail, just keeping in touch,
Scheduling a meeting, let's do lunch, a friend.

What was he thinking?
What has he ever been thinking?
Once more to touch a heart.
It's the dance of the foolish old man.

He lives in his prime, doesn't see the change.
The years of pain, the losses in love and war,
He's accepted them, learned from them, grown with each scar,
And yet…there is more…there must be more.

The hope never dies, the dreams stay alive, love is always new,
The world he writes, the world inside his head,
That state of being, just beyond comprehension, defying expression,
Is always nearby at the dance of the foolish old man.

Ghosts

Once again the world grows cold.
The ghosts return from the attic, from behind the drapes,
Where I had banished them so little time ago.

You knew we'd be back. We'll always be with you.

Yes, I knew.
Like the brief remission of pain that plagued my life,
Till the doctors drilled into my skull,
Your absence was temporary.
I knew that from the beginning.
And yet, you were gone so totally,
While sunshine poured through the window,
And joy flowed from me.
It was never what it seemed,
It was simply what I needed to survive,
A moment so connected with the world,
That it let me live again.

You should never have sent us away. Do we need to remind you?

You remind me every day.
Since the day my brother died.
There is no turning back. There is no second chance.
And again, when my wife died,
And again, my mother,
And the many loves who passed through my life unremarked,
As I guarded against unbearable loss.

And now?

You are, at least, ghosts that I understand.
I will not open the curtains again.
You are my psychic tape worm.
I will feed you pain, and you will leave me alone.
Most nights.

Siena
□□□

Tuscan summer
The taste of your kiss lingers
Only in my mind

Perfect parallel
Touch and go. Life changed always
My Siena dream

Silence speaks
A language of its own
Eloquent and spare

Refraction

This is the best one. I caught it myself. I got lots of bites, but this is the Biggest and best. It's a queen. I named it after you.

The In Basket

□□□

LAYER
upon
LAYER
upon
LAYER
upon
LAYER
upon
LAYER
of
EVERYDAY MINUTIAE

CONFOUNDS

creativity
FRUSTRATES
fulfillment
IMOBILIZES
initiative
and makes even the
POET
wax
TRITE

-- IN --

The Zoophabet

Rhythmic Rhyme at Story Time

A

An aardvark named Avery,
Craved ants that were savory,
And went to extremes to obtain them,
She shipped them air cargo,
From Northwest Key Largo,
And then couldn't wait to deplane them.

B

Brianna was a woolly bear,
Out strolling in her underwear,
She asked an eagle flying by,
How far it was up to the sky,
The eagle said, "You'll know as soon,
As monkeys fly around the moon."

C

I saw a caterpillar on the handle of a tiller,
On a ship that I saw sailing by the shore,
But by late that afternoon, there was just an old cocoon,
And the caterpillar wasn't anymore.

D

A dusty old dingo that nobody knew,
Danced to the tune of a didgeridoo,
And all of the wallabies hopped around singing,
And dreamed of the rain that the springtime was bringing.

E

An elephant named Evan goes to school every day,
He is round around the middle, but he loves to run and play,
In the night when no one's looking he puts on a tennis shoe,
And he dances in a circle cause it's what he likes to do.

F

A frog is just a frog is just a frog and not a prince,
Oh sure, he'll tell you stories and he'll drop a lot of hints,
He'll say he's waiting for a lady's kiss to break the curse,
And you'll think that though he's warty you have kissed a whole lot worse,
So you'll pucker up and smooch him with your hands upon your hips,
Then once again he'll leave, cause you have warts upon your lips.

G

The silliness of Emma's gibbons,
Is that they like to play with ribbons,
They all go sailing through the air,
With streamers streaming from their hair.

H

I don't know why folks make a fuss,
About a hippopotamus,
They have no culture or tradition,
And have a nasty disposition,
They eat sea grass, their breath is stale,
They swish their potty with their tail,
If I would ever have a hippo,
I think that I would name him "Zippo."

I

Iguanas are groovy, they're black, red or green,
And scaly and pointy and oddly serene,
They nibble the algae wherever it grows,
Then bask in the sun and blow salt from their nose.
If I could do anything now that I wanna,
I'd trade in my cat for a neat green iguana.

J

Jackalopes are very rare,
You hardly see them anywhere,
With big brown ears and eyes of red,
And hat racks mounted on their heads,
But here's a card that shows them hopping,
"Hi from Texas. Thanks for stopping!"

K

A kangaroo has lots to do,
She has to hurry right along,
There's grass to graze and kids to raise,
And parties at the billabong.

L

The lamprey has a scary look, she has a toothy grin,
She lives inside a coral cave and lures the fishes in,
She sets out cakes and cookies and she plays a big bassoon,
Then she tells a silly story of the setting of the moon,
She dresses up in lavender and wears a frilly hat,
Oh I wish that I could be an eel and have such fun as that.

M

Morgan Mongoose has a job and really needs a break,
She has to stay up every night to eat another snake,
The Kylie snake's her favorite from Bombay to Bangalore,
But she did her job so well there are no Kylies anymore.

N

The nightingale sings like a lark,
To lovers wooing in the park,
His evening song seems just as sweet,
To others who are less discreet,
But best of all his song may sail,
Off to a lady nightingale.

O

Opossums are marsupials and when the kids are small,
They ride inside a pouch that has a spigot on the wall,
But when the kids have left the house and ma is all alone,
She has an extra pocket where she stores her keys and phone.

P

Amanda the Panda is really a sight,
She's totally black, except where she's white.
She was totally bored with nothing to do,
But wander the hills and eat shoots of bamboo,
So she called for a cab and she rode into town,
Where she hired a rickshaw to take her around,
To a nice Chinese place where she ate up a platter
Of leaves and small sticks and some vegetable matter,
Then she grabbed a revolver and shot out the light,
And ran through the doorway and into the night.
Now you may think that's rude, but you know that it's true,
That animals do what they're programmed to do,
The mocking bird mocks and retrievers retrieve,
And the Way of the Panda? It eats shoots and leaves.

Q

Quetzals are gorgeous in green, red and blue,
Sitting high in the branches with little to do,
They nibble on guava and sometimes on mango,
And late in the evening I've heard that they tango.

R

Raccoons are suspicious and always wear masks,
But they're really inventive and have secret tasks,
They have secret code names, they're "Hollys" and "Jasons,"
And secret societies just like the Masons,
They talk secret language and hang with their chums,
Just think what they'd do with opposable thumbs.

S

My father is a seahorse so of course I call him Mummy,
He always has me with him in a pouch outside his tummy,
The other fish have said it's not a macho thing, it's true,
But I love my manly Mummy and no other dad would do.

T

When TE the tiger roars loud in the night,
The villagers hide in their houses in fright,
They think he will eat them, but chances are slim,
Cause he's roaring with laughter. I'm tickling him.

U

My good friend Asher blows his horn,
To summon up his unicorn,
Then saddles up and pretty soon,
They'll fly across the harvest moon.
Or slide down rainbows in the sky,
Or play with eagles way up high,
They've been that way since they were born,
Have Asher and his unicorn.

V

The vicuña is a camelid with long and silky hair,
He lives up in the Andes where there's very little air,
His cousin's a guanaco and his grandpa's likely llama,
Do you suppose he could have had alpaca for a mama?

W

Wally was a warthog, with tusks of gleaming white,
He brushed them in the morning and he brushed again at night,
He flossed them both at midnight, he polished in the rain,
And he had the brightest smile on the Serengeti plain.

X

Xenopus toads with clawed back feet are also called platannas,
They live in southern Africa and never eat bananas,
Their skin is awfully slimy and they haven't got a tongue,
How can they lick an ice cream cone or holler at their young?

Y

I'm heavy and I'm woolly and I like it in the snow,
I'm never in a hurry cause I've got no place to go,
I huddle with my buddies with the cold wind at my back,
But I have a PhD cause I'm the world's smartest yak.

Z

Zebras have a choice to make each day when sleep is done,
Which suit to wear while roaming the savannah in the sun.
The black one with the white stripes is really debonair,
The white one with the black stripes is also nice to wear,
But how's a zebra to decide which one is wrong or right,
When the white and black ensemble looks just like the black and white?

LMRX

A learned professor from Emory,
Declaimed on his marvelous memory,
"Every fact that I've read,
Has a place in my head,
From August clear through to Septemory."

On a hot, humid night in Ceylon,
A Tamil with too little on,
Tried to dance cheek to cheek,
With a Turk and a Sikh,
And a queen and a duke and a pawn.

A Shakespearean actor once found,
An old Indian burial mound,
Climbing up, spake, "It's clear to me,
I must spout a soliloquy,
On the brave's grave that's under this ground."

A debate between two hippopotami,
Revolved around how best to swat a fly,
Said the crusty old male,
"With a flip of my tail,
I can flatten them all and they're bound to die."

A thoughtful blond princess from Malibu,
Created a surf board with Super Glue,
Then with one final drop,
Stuck her I-Pad on top,
So she surfed from the shore when she wanted to.

A Valentine's Poem

Each year I start to write this rhyme,
That's never done in Valen-time,
Cause I can't find the words to say,
"I love you" in a different way.

Seems all the words were said before,
By wandering knights in days of yore,
By Indians in a birch canoe,
By Maughams and paupers, children, too,

By Slavic folks from Budapest,
By hired hands who need a rest,
By astronauts up on the moon,
And bureaucrats who nap at noon.

From kings and princes, knights and knaves,
To first assistant galley slaves,
We all have summoned up the Muse,
To find the words to write the news:

That love has filled us with desire,
And left us with our pants on fire.
When hormone levels start to rise,
We're all romantic kind of guys.

A Valentines Poem -1993

I thought that it would be just fine, if I wrote you a Valentine,
A simple verse and nothing more, the kind of thing I've done before.
But Monday when I tried to rhyme, I thought I had a lot of time,
So when I tired, I went to bed. I should have worked on words instead.

Then Tuesday when I tried again, the words kept sticking to my pen,
They *dragged* and **smeared** and made a *mess*.
 .....I gave up Tuesday, I confess.
On Wednesday I was doing fine, until I spilled my glass of wine.
Inspiration's hard to get, when all your words are blurred and wet.

Thursday night was worst of all: my writing crashed into the wall!
Left every mote of meter mangled, every participle dangled.
Friday found the pressure on, every hope of victory gone,
It left me just one thing to do: go buy a Hallmark card for you.

The Hallmark owner was away. His clerk had left for France that day,
So in the country's finest mall, I couldn't find a card at all.
And that's my story, mostly true, or else I'd have a card for you.
A card that said, in words so fine, "Won't you be my Valentine?"

Mango Dreams

It must have been the mango that woke me up last night.
The duck and lamb were excellent, asparagus just right,
The mushrooms in the rice were not the psychedelic kind,
But well before the light of dawn strange visions filled my mind.

The fragments of forgotten verse, song titles never used,
Began to march around my head, and kept themselves amused,
By prying up my eyelids and diving in my brain,
Playing hide-and-seek among the pleasure and the pain.

They kicked up dust from dustbins of forgotten histories,
Creating psychic sneezing fits from Freudian allergies,
With evanescent images what weren't quite what they seem,
Your visage formed and faded and became a separate dream.

But mango dreams continued as the night marched coldly on,
With songs and memories melding, then melting into dawn.
A couple cups of coffee and I'll be back from the dead,
But echoes of these mango dreams still ring within my head.

Mothers' Day

It's Mother's Day again, My Dear. (It happens this way every year.),
You're not my mom; the children know I happened many years ago,
So I don't have to send a card, or plant a flower in your yard,
Or bring you breakfast to your bed. The kids can do that stuff instead.

You didn't know me as a tyke, or teach me how to ride a bike,
Or bring me home a dog named Spot, or wrap the toys that Santa brought.
While I grew up, it wasn't you who dried my tears and tied my shoe,
But Mom was there to hear my prayers, and keep me safe from bats and bears.

When I was scared, she'd hold me tight, and pretty soon I'd lose my fright.
Who knew where next year's home would be - in Washington or Germany,
Just one sure thing: where ere we'd roam, wherever there was Morn, was home.

So I'll call Mom before it's late, and tell her that I think she's great.
Our kids I'm sure will both have fun and make you feel you're Number One,
I'll bet they made some cards for you with doilies, string, and Elmer's glue.

And though we're half a world apart, I'll share with you what's in my heart:
In thinking of my mom this way, I see the things you do each day,
The love you give the kids and me, that binds us as a family.

It hurts because I couldn't say some special thing this special day,
I wish that I could write a song of how you've made our children strong,
Of all the times you've dried their tears, and shed your own across the years.

I'd write a poem so you would know the reasons that I love you so
Include the fact that you're a mother who isn't quite like any other,
And anywhere that we may roam, as long as you're the mom, I'm home.

Maddie McGuire

Maddie McFadden McTavish McGuire,
Distressed all her friends with a diet quite dire.
She wasn't too young and she wasn't too old,
She wasn't too meek and she wasn't too bold,
She did almost everything she had been told,

Except when it came to her everyday meal,
The everyday food didn't have an appeal, so…

She wouldn't eat carrots or cabbage or kale,
She wouldn't eat tuna or turkey or whale,
She wouldn't eat peaches or pears for a snack,
She wouldn't eat walrus or weasel or yak.

She didn't eat lemons, she didn't eat limes,
She couldn't eat nuts, though she tried several times,
She didn't eat pork and she didn't eat peas,
She only ate mumbling bumbling bees.

They sometimes objected, and sometimes they stung,
And she always had pollen all over her tongue,
But they're all she would eat, and they kept her alive,
Until that sad day when she emptied the hive.

But no one was worried, because they all knew,
She'd eat hot dogs and bagels and maybe a stew,
Yes, when she got hungry, she'd eat like the rest,
The fruits and the veggies she used to detest.

They knew she'd eat cheeseburgers, blintzes and fries,
Instead of just bees, and occasional flies.
But Maddie surprised them, she wouldn't eat food,
If she couldn't have bees, she was not in the mood.

So the neighbors all panicked, and offered large bounties,
To locate new bee hives in neighboring counties.
But the word had leaked out, and the local bees knew,
That Maddie was hungry. They got up and flew.

And they hid in the clover just north of Nepal,
Where they stayed through the summer, and into the fall,
And Maddie – thank goodness – her stubborn streak broke,
Now she eats only eggs…but she won't touch the yolks!

A Haiku in the Woods
□ □ □

Desert in turmoil
The Turtle speaks Arabic
Have him fly gliders

Chickadee in web
Spider approaching with care
Who is kidding whom?

No crisis today
Far too much free time at work
Need adrenalin

Letters on my desk
"Thank you" in twelve languages
Babel's tower down

Running shoes unworn
Air pure, sky clear, no excuse
The road mocks me still

Caffeinated cat
Tail twitches, rides with witches
Should have bought a dog

Farewells

It's only plastic, not like a real ant farm. I got all these ants in the back yard. Someday I'll have a real ant farm. Ant farms are pretty dumb anyway.

Thantos

The specter of thy beauty wends its way on lonely nights,
Across the years and twisted miles into my troubled mind,
And lightly there, surcease it brings as life's deceits unwind,
Till stretching out my longing arms, I chase you from my sight.

Ah, that the years could fall away, and that we two could find,
Our place among the garden walks in morning's blissful glow,
And once again walk hand in hand where flashing fountains flow,
To wash away the worldly woes of reeling wretched mind.

But, no! The sinner pays the price, and still beneath the snow
Thy beauty uncorrupted lies where verdant virgins sleep,
While mortified and more than dead, this burning mortal weeps,
And turns his hopes from heaven to the burning brimstone glow,

To the seething, suffering turmoil of the damned immortal keep,
No more a hell than life on earth where grimly death doth reap.

92

It doesn't really matter what I see when I look in your eyes.
It is not what you see when you look in the mirror.
What I see in you exists only in my mind,
And hidden in your heart.

Are you afraid to see in you what I see?
Are you afraid to accept the you I hold in my heart?
Can you give me your hand? Your trust? Your heart?
Where are you tonight?

As I look at the stars,
And breathe the lonely silence,
Of the star-filled night,
Could I hold you with my eyes?

Or do you run ahead of the fire?
I watch, and transcend the years,
As if patience will bring peace,
And fidelity will bring love.

Death Take the Final Scene

The world's a stage, an endless stream
Of paupers low and mean,
Borne into life to end a life,
Death take the final scene.

The world is gray, a formless void
Of acts obscure, obscene,
Borne slowly by the stream of Life
Till Death, the final scene.

The world may yet have form of sorts,
A night with days between,
Yet through the day, the specter still
Of Death , the final scene.

What is the Sun without its Warmth?

What is the sun without its warmth?
It is the golden edifice, now empty,
    From which dreams once flowed.
It is the aching hands, now numb,
    The longing arms, now lame,
    The burning heart, now cold,
        That for one glorious instant in
        Eternity were kindled by the
        Warmth of that now cold sun,
        Into a force so intense that it will
        Outlive the memory of man.

What is a union without its union?
It is one mind, now two,
    One heart, now two,
It is one man whose hopes and fears,
    Joys and tears,
    Needs and passions,
        Must live within his own soul
        Lest the light of his sun
        Be kept forever
        From his blinded eyes.

If we get to the end of the road

If we get to the end of the road and you find that I am not there,
Look back with fondness at our pages of moonlit images,
And remember how far we walked together,
How you held my hand when the lions roared around us,
How we kept each other warm for a moment in a cold and bitter night,
Just warm enough to go on.

Night

The night races on.
In desolation I cry for you,
In desperation I seek the solace of sleep.
Nothingness. No beginning, no end,
And in the middle,
A world of hanging mats and marshmallow cream
To be sloshed through.
A labyrinth of formless sacks
Chasing me through a child's dream.
My childhood dream.
Candy canes at Christmas,
Only when I'm sick.
And what is sick?
Days in bed with aspirin?
Days in bed with the butcher's wife?
Days as Peter, nights as Paul?
Sleep!

...the now

But now, always I feel the truth,
And I burst from within myself,
To know that what I feel to be,
Is not exactly the perfect thing.

Tenderness I take much,
And try to make that happiness.
Now, this will reach me,
Your touch will tell.

So much in the way of love,
To know and understand and bless.
But to understand happiness
Is freshness and new delight.

As I gaze out into the blue circles of your eyes' truth,
To me come the real images of light and darkness and days forever,
The perfect solid love so bright as to make the night,
The day's most precious possession.

Are you fact or fantasy

Are you fact of fantasy,
You who guides my pen,
Who paints my strings with melody,
Who puts the song in the rain?

Could Fact touch so deeply, hurt so sublimely?
Could it be so constant in the telling and the retelling?
Or could Fantasy have your frailties, your searching soul,
Your need for…something unknown?

You are, perhaps both:
A fact that touches my body; a spirit that touches my soul.
You are a part of my being, a part of my reality.
As surely as the face in the mirror, you are with me constantly.

All the words unspoken

All the words unspoken
Burning in my heart
Promise madness in the night
Tearing me apart

Every chance encounter
Every time I call
Puts me closer to the edge
Closer to the fall

Polac Cloj

Here I stand, alone and cold.
My only friend the endless road,
    If sometime in the future years
    My thinking clears
    I dry my tears
Perhaps we'll share my load.

But just for now, I think I'll stay
Alone and lonely; it's my way
    To find my peace the way
    I deem the best,
    To sit alone and dream,
From night to near-night, day.

For dreams are friends that never fail
To show us in the victor's mail,
    In truth I lost the purest part,
    I gave my love,
    I lost my heart,
And fell as chaff on shale.

And now you say that you love me,
That being one will set us free,
    If sometime in the future years
    My thinking clears,
    I lose my fears,
    Forget the sear of burning tears,
I'll come back home and see.

Blind Men

Blind men.
Standing face to face in a blackened room,
Holding death in their hands.
Deaf men.
Sitting side by side in a silent room,
Holding fear in their hearts.
Numb men.
Staying miles apart in a barren room,
Holding nothing in their lives.

Blind men.
Blinded by ignorance, hatred, and fear,
Ready to lash out and kill.
Deaf men.
Unwilling to listen to the cries of an aching world,
Entombment self-imposed.
Numb men.
Unable to touch each other's hand,
To set themselves free.

When first I felt the breeze caress my face

When first I felt the breeze caress my face
I turned to look in wonder through sun-lit silence,
And saw your eyes.
They haunt me still.

Your smile I beheld as in a dream.
I lived on your laughter,
Heard through an eternity
Of breathless pain.

In the echoes of a thousand churches,
The heartache of a thousand years,
The dust of a thousand dreams,
I trace the passage of my tears.

At Night She Cries

"I feel fine," she says, "Much better than last time.
My hair isn't even falling out. We're gonna beat this thing."
You bet. You rock, Girl. So she smiles, gets back to work,
Solves other people's problems, answers e-mail, comforts the kids.

"The coughing is just a springtime allergy; a little tired, not sleeping well,
The doctor will give me something for that. Chemo's just for a while."
The phone rings, another caring friend needing to be comforted,
And she is again the comforter, assuring everyone things will be all right.

But at night she cries. When the phones have gone to sleep,
And the lights are at rest, and she is alone with her man,
She cries in his arms. She is tired, she is sick,
Food has no taste, she gets confused and forgets why it's worth the fight.

He tries to comfort her, tries to say the right things,
Tells her they'll get through this together,
And he believes what he says, though his heart is filled with fear,
And his own tears have fallen where she cannot see.

She loves him because he tries so hard,
She loves him because he is her strength,
But she hates that he will not see she is dying,
And that secret is a cancer of its own.

We come into the world surrounded by a mother's love.
And travel for a time in the company of friends,
But the last few steps are a journey of a singular nature,
One we must each take alone.

I lost my faith along that road, but for you,
If you find in your solitude that God is walking quietly beside you,
Put your hand in His, take Him into your heart,
And He will lead you home.

Here I am

Here I am,
With everything to give.
Who will take?

Who has walked my path,
And has seen what I have seen?
Who can believe what I know?
Would I, had I not seen?

Hold the hand I reach out to you,
Dry the tears in my heart.
And all that I am or ever will be is yours.

Epilogue

A Prayer on Parting

As I reach out this hand to touch your face,
Time-worn with love, I see another face,
Warm with the glow of expectant youth.

I see a face — looking through a half century of memories —
In a school yard in Spring: a young woman,
Wearing my sweater and holding my hand.

I see a face forty years gone by,
Holding a baby, washing her messy face;
The shine a little burnished, perhaps, but with so much love.

I see, through three decades, a face
Full of excitement for a daughter's first prom,
Waiting with me late into a Spring night, till she should return.

I see a face of twenty years past,
Holding our first grandchild,
With the tenderness that only you could give.

And ten years ago — it seems like only a heartbeat —
I see you over this space, too: sitting by the fire
Your eyes warm with the talk of yesterday and tomorrow.

Now I touch your face again, as I have ten thousand times before.
And the love in my touch could be no greater,
If the fires of hell were paled by my passion.

My love for you is not that of our youth, or that of our middle years.
It is the sum of everything we have been and hoped for,
The joy and pain, the delight of a lifetime with you.

And if tomorrow we are not blessed to be together, let there always be this:
For you, the memory of the feeling in this touch.
For me, the great joy of having loved you.

Charles Bridge, 1993

□ □ □

I have an ant farm. Wanta see my ant farm? I bought it with my own money. Saved all summer. Wanna see my ant farm?

I have some poetry in a folder. It is all that I am. I keep it in this folder,
In the dark, like I keep me. Could I share this with you?

******** ******* ******

This is the best one. I caught it myself. I got lots of bites, but this is the Biggest and best. It's a queen. I named it after you.

I have a new song. If you like I'll play it for you. I wrote it for you.
There's no magic in the words or music, but it helps me hold on to the feelings
That are so fleeting, and so precious. Feelings that you awaken in me.

******** ******* ******

It's only plastic, not like a real ant farm. I got all these ants in the back yard. Someday I'll have a real ant farm. Ant farms are pretty dumb anyway.

This isn't great stuff. I just write it for me. It's just therapy, really.
The rest of that is old stuff. Pretty strange. Here, let me put this away.

www.ingramcontent.com/pod-product-compliance
Lightning Source LLC
Chambersburg PA
CBHW032149040426
42449CB00005B/451